CONTENTS

INTRODUCTION

Buckingham Palace serves as both an official home and an office for The Queen. It is the setting for state ceremonies and official entertaining and is one of the few working royal palaces remaining in the world today. In the Middle Ages the London residence of the Norman and Plantagenet kings and their successors was the Palace of Westminster, now rebuilt as the Houses of Parliament. Whitehall was the main royal palace from the reign of Henry VIII to that of William III, when it was largely destroyed by fire. In the eighteenth century St James's Palace, built by Henry VIII

BELOW: Detail of map of Cities of London and Westminster, 1799 by Richard Horwood, showing Buckingham House

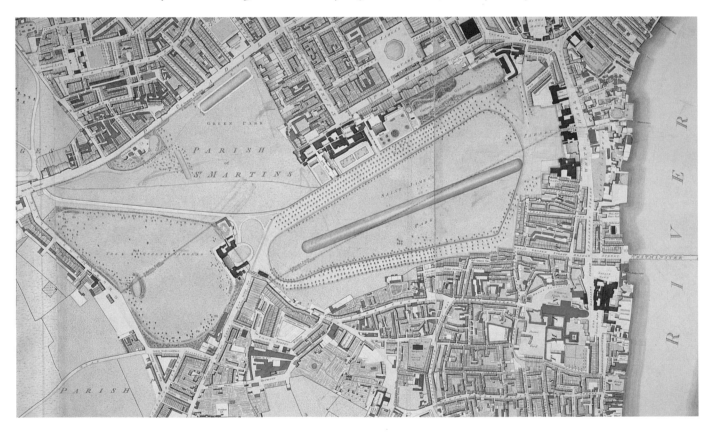

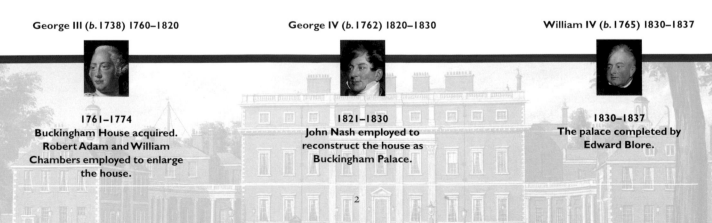

George III (b. 1738) 1760–1820

1761–1774
Buckingham House acquired. Robert Adam and William Chambers employed to enlarge the house.

George IV (b. 1762) 1820–1830

1821–1830
John Nash employed to reconstruct the house as Buckingham Palace.

William IV (b. 1765) 1830–1837

1830–1837
The palace completed by Edward Blore.

INTRODUCTION

on the site of a medieval leper hospital to serve as a hunting lodge, was used by the Hanoverian kings. The creation of Buckingham Palace as an appropriate symbol of national greatness in the aftermath of the victories of the Napoleonic Wars was due to George IV.

Although converted to a palace by George IV and first lived in by Queen Victoria soon after her accession in 1837, the property was acquired originally for the Crown by George III in 1761. The history of the site, however, can be traced back to the beginning of the seventeenth century. In 1633 Lord Goring built on it 'a fair house and other convenient buildings and outhouses'. The house was rebuilt for John Sheffield, Duke of Buckingham, in 1702–5 by the architect William Winde.

The most attractive feature of the house was its setting between St James's Park and Hyde Park, at the head of an avenue of limes and elms with views towards Westminster and the City of London and with the dome of St Paul's visible in the distance. It was more

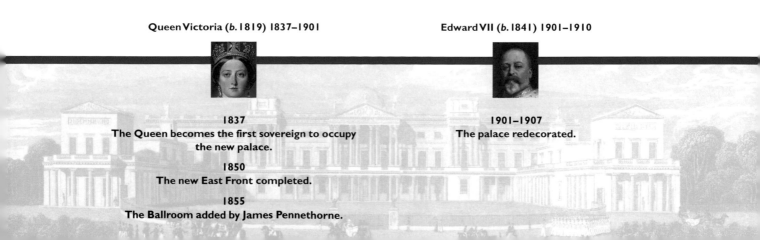

Queen Victoria (b. 1819) 1837–1901

Edward VII (b. 1841) 1901–1910

1837
The Queen becomes the first sovereign to occupy the new palace.

1901–1907
The palace redecorated.

1850
The new East Front completed.

1855
The Ballroom added by James Pennethorne.

LEFT: *George III, Queen Charlotte and their Six Eldest Children* by Johann Zoffany, 1770

a country house on the edge of London than a town house, and to some extent it has retained this character ever since.

Buckingham House remained the property of the Dukes of Buckingham – after whom it was named – until the mid-eighteenth century. A problem over the lease of the property, half of which was on Crown land, enabled George III to acquire it in 1761 as a private residence following his marriage to Charlotte of Mecklenburg-Strelitz. Between 1762 and 1774 Buckingham House was remodelled by Sir William Chambers. The ceremonial centre of the court remained at St James's, resulting in the anomaly whereby foreign ambassadors are still accredited to the Court of St James more than two centuries later.

When George IV came to the throne in 1820, he decided to redesign Buckingham Palace as his own residence for use in conjunction with St James's, as in his father's day, but by 1826 he opted instead to convert it into a full-scale palace where he could hold his courts and conduct the official business of the monarchy.

King George V (b. 1865) 1910–1936   **Edward VIII (b. 1894) 1936**

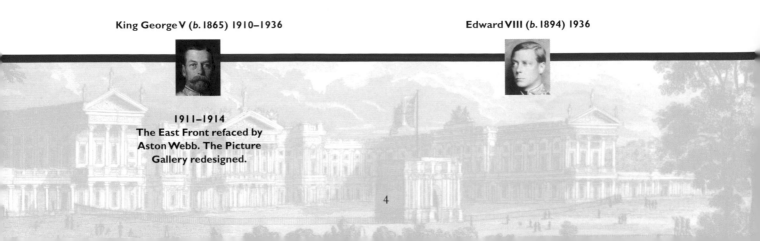

1911–1914
The East Front refaced by Aston Webb. The Picture Gallery redesigned.

He chose as his architect John Nash, whose design for the new palace was theatrical and French-inspired, perfectly reflecting George IV's personal taste. Nash was hampered, however, by the ambivalence of intention over the purpose of the palace – whether it was to be a private royal residence or a state palace – as well as by shortage of funds. He was forced to keep and remodel the old house. To this day the shell of the Duke of Buckingham's and George III's house is incorporated in the middle of the principal range of the palace. It dictates the plan and dimensions of the rooms and the proportions of the ground floor.

Nevertheless, Nash's plan was an ingenious solution to a difficult architectural problem. The main block was doubled in size by the addition of new rooms on the garden side. The old wings were demolished and replaced by new ones to form a solid U-shape enclosing an open courtyard, the fourth side of which was finished with iron railings and a central triumphal arch. The old main block was remodelled,

ABOVE: *Buckingham Palace from the South East* by Joseph Nash, 1846. The Marble Arch, now at the top of Park Lane, can be seen in its original position at the entrance to the forecourt

King George VI (b. 1895) 1936–1952

Queen Elizabeth II (b. 1926) 1952–

1940–1942
The palace bombed nine times.

1962
The Queen's Gallery opened.

1993
Buckingham Palace opened to the public in August and September for the first time.

permitting both a circuit of the State Rooms and an axial approach to the Throne Room within the shell of the Duke of Buckingham's house. This made the new State Rooms on the first floor equally suitable for formal audiences and for more social court events.

The exterior of Nash's palace, faced in Bath stone, is exquisitely detailed in a French Neo-classical manner making much use of sculptured panels and trophies, while the main feature of the garden front was a domed semi-circular bow.

The interiors of the palace were progressively enriched by George IV with the advice of his artistic 'guru' Sir Charles Long, to meet an increasing desire for opulence and grandeur. The decoration was notable for its large-scale use of brightly coloured scagliola, lapis blue and raspberry pink; the sculptured plaster panels set high up; and the elaborately decorated ceilings. George IV died before the rooms were finished.

The completion of the palace was entrusted by William IV to Edward Blore, a more businesslike but far less inspired architect. In general he kept to the lines of Nash's design, but made it more solid and less picturesque.

William IV never lived in Buckingham Palace, though it was completed in his reign. In 1837, when Queen Victoria moved in, the

BELOW: The East Front, mid-1870s, showing Edward Blore's original façade, subsequently refaced by Sir Aston Webb

RIGHT: The Royal Air Force
Fly Past to mark the end of
the annual celebration of The
Queen's Official Birthday

palace was fresh from the hands of the builders, but its inadequacies
became obvious following the Queen's marriage to her cousin, Prince
Albert of Saxe-Coburg, in 1840. The root of the trouble was that
the palace was too small, both for state functions and for family life.
Splendid though George IV's State Apartments were, none of them
was big enough for a court ball. Equally serious for the newly mar-
ried couple was the absence of nurseries. The obvious solution was
to make the palace a complete quadrangle by closing the east side
of the courtyard with a new wing. This scheme was adopted, entail-
ing the removal of the Marble Arch.

INTRODUCTION

LEFT: The Centre Room, from which members of the Royal Family emerge to wave from the Balcony to the crowds after ceremonial occasions

ABOVE: The Queen and members of the Royal Family on the Balcony

The new range, with the necessary apartments for distinguished visitors on the first floor and nurseries on top, was designed by Edward Blore and built by Thomas Cubitt from 1847 to 1850.

The extension of the suite of State Apartments along the west front of the palace by the addition at the south end of new galleries, the State Supper Room and the huge Ballroom, 40 metres [123 feet] long and 20 metres [60 feet] wide, was entrusted to a different architect, Nash's pupil James Pennethorne.

During the long years of her widowhood Queen Victoria spent more time at Windsor Castle, and Buckingham Palace remained dark and shuttered for most of the year. When Edward VII came to the throne in 1901, he considered the redecoration of the palace 'a duty and necessity'. The Ballroom, Grand Entrance, Marble Hall, Grand Staircase, vestibules and galleries were all painted white, heavily gilded, and embellished with finicky festoons, swags and other decorative motifs at odds with Nash's original detailing.

For the east range Blore had used soft Caen stone which proved to be perishable in the London climate. During the reign of King George V, in 1913, the Blore front was therefore refaced in Portland stone to a new design by Aston Webb as part of the Queen Victoria Memorial; the remodelled approach along the Mall, planned in 1901, was completed at the same time.

It is owing to Webb that Buckingham Palace looks like everybody's idea of a palace. Much of the architectural effect comes from the forecourt and new *rond point* in front, with magnificent gateways and railings, the gilded ironwork of which was made by the Bromsgrove Guild.

PLAN OF THE STATE ROOMS

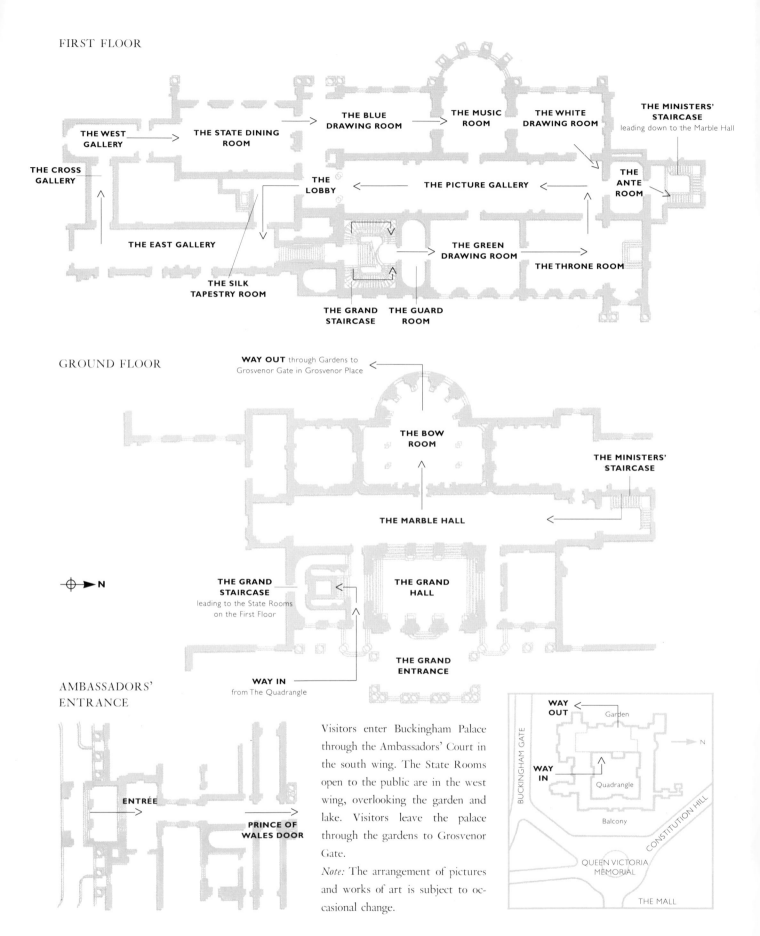

FIRST FLOOR

THE WEST GALLERY

THE STATE DINING ROOM

THE BLUE DRAWING ROOM

THE MUSIC ROOM

THE WHITE DRAWING ROOM

THE MINISTERS' STAIRCASE
leading down to the Marble Hall

THE CROSS GALLERY

THE LOBBY

THE PICTURE GALLERY

THE ANTE ROOM

THE EAST GALLERY

THE GREEN DRAWING ROOM

THE THRONE ROOM

THE SILK TAPESTRY ROOM

THE GRAND STAIRCASE

THE GUARD ROOM

GROUND FLOOR

WAY OUT through Gardens to Grosvenor Gate in Grosvenor Place

THE BOW ROOM

THE MINISTERS' STAIRCASE

THE MARBLE HALL

N

THE GRAND STAIRCASE
leading to the State Rooms on the First Floor

THE GRAND HALL

THE GRAND ENTRANCE

WAY IN
from The Quadrangle

AMBASSADORS' ENTRANCE

ENTRÉE

PRINCE OF WALES DOOR

WAY OUT Garden

BUCKINGHAM GATE

WAY IN Quadrangle

N

CONSTITUTION HILL

Balcony

QUEEN VICTORIA MEMORIAL

THE MALL

Visitors enter Buckingham Palace through the Ambassadors' Court in the south wing. The State Rooms open to the public are in the west wing, overlooking the garden and lake. Visitors leave the palace through the gardens to Grosvenor Gate.

Note: The arrangement of pictures and works of art is subject to occasional change.

INTRODUCTION TO THE STATE ROOMS

The State Rooms, which form the backdrop to the pageantry of court ceremonial and official entertaining, occupy the main west block facing the gardens.

Unlike many other historic monuments, Buckingham Palace remains a fully occupied, working royal palace and this gives it a particular fascination. The Queen, as Head of State, receives there a large number of formal and informal visitors, including the Prime Minister at weekly audiences, the Privy Council, foreign and British ambassadors and high commissioners, bishops, and senior officers of the armed services and the civil service. There are regular Investitures in the Ballroom. Each autumn The Queen gives a splendid formal reception in the State Rooms for all members of the diplomatic corps in London. Three times a year, in the summer, Garden Parties are held which are attended by a wide range of guests including MPs, clergy and those active in local and public life, amounting to 27,000 people in all. The practice of holding small, private lunch parties for guests drawn from leaders in the community is an innovation of the present reign.

The highlight of royal entertaining, however, is the State Banquet, usually for about 170 guests, given by The Queen on the first evening of a State Visit by a foreign Head of State to the United Kingdom. At Buckingham Palace, State Banquets are held in the Ballroom, the largest of the State Rooms, using the magnificent gold plate from the Royal Collection, much of it made for George IV. Guests are received in the Music Room and after they have taken their places at table a royal procession is formed to the Ballroom, led by The Queen and the visiting Head of State and preceded by the Lord Chamberlain and the Lord Steward, who both walk backwards.

In all, Buckingham Palace has 19 state rooms, 52 royal and guest bedrooms, 188 staff bedrooms, 92 offices and 78 bathrooms. Some 450 people work in the palace and more than 50,000 people are entertained there every year.

The Lord Chamberlain is the head of the Household, responsible for running the palace and organising the court ceremonial, as well as the upkeep of the palace and its collections. Under him are the heads of various departments, who include the Crown Equerry – in charge of the Mews; the Keeper of the Privy Purse; and the Master of the Household, a position dating back to 1539, who is responsible for the organisation of official entertaining.

THE AMBASSADORS' ENTRANCE

LEFT: The Ambassadors' Entrance

Visitors enter the palace from Buckingham Gate through the Ambassadors' Court. The Ambassadors' Entrance is a temple-like Ionic portico of Bath stone on the south side of the palace. It was added under the direction of Edward Blore after Nash had been dismissed as architect of the palace in 1830, but takes its cue from the Nash conservatories on the garden front (one of which is now The Queen's Gallery, with changing exhibitions from the Royal Collection). This is the entrance used on official occasions by the diplomats and others with similar privileges. The hall itself is a narrow space, known as the Entrée, lined with marbled pilasters. The Brocatello chimney-piece and the mirror over it are insertions in the seventeenth-century style dating from when the Entrée was redecorated in 1924, and bear the monogram of King George V. The mirror incorporates a gilded sunburst clock, its dial encircled by the Garter.

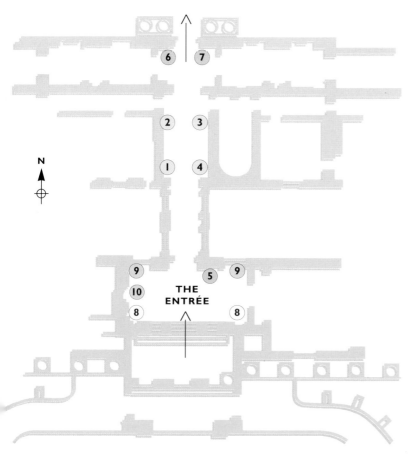

PICTURES

1 *George II* by John Shackleton, 1757

2 *George I* by George Wilhelm Fountaine, c. 1725

3 *Queen Victoria* by Sir George Hayter, c. 1840

4 *Frederick, Prince of Wales*, Anonymous, British School, c. 1745

SCULPTURE

5 John McCombe Reynolds, Bronze bust of HM The Queen, 1984

6 Sir Francis Chantrey, *Arthur, 1st Duke of Wellington*, 1837

7 E. Davis, *Victoria, Duchess of Kent*, 1843

FURNITURE

8 Pair of French patinated and gilt bronze candelabra, late 18th century; on English giltwood tripod torchères, early 19th century

PORCELAIN

9 Pair of Chinese celadon vases with gilt bronze mounts attributed to the Vulliamys, c. 1810

10 Cistern. Chinese *famille rose*, with gilt bronze mounts, attributed to Benjamin Lewis Vulliamy, c. 1820

THE GRAND ENTRANCE

In the Quadrangle the visitor first savours the impact of Nash's architecture for George IV. Here all seems to be golden Bath stone, but Edward Blore's surviving rear elevation of the east range is actually stuccoed and painted stone colour, while the lower columns are of cast iron, also painted. The quality of George IV's concept is apparent in the large but elegant double portico with its superimposed columns, stoutly Doric at ground-floor level and richly Corinthian above, influenced by Claude Perrault's design for the Louvre portico in Paris.

An important feature of the original design of Buckingham Palace was the programme of integrated sculptural ornament intended to display contemporary artistic talent. It reflects the early nineteenth-century enthusiasm for British art, manifested also in the array of marble monuments to national heroes in St Paul's Cathedral. John Flaxman, the greatest of English Neo-classical sculptors, was first approached to design the carved decorations. But he died in 1826 after making sketches for the external sculpture which was executed by other hands. The beautifully moulded capitals and friezes are of Coade stone (a type of terracotta popularised in the eighteenth century by Mrs Eleanor Coade), supplied by William Croggan in 1827. Croggan also made the original crowning figures of *Neptune, Commerce* and *Navigation* (now removed). In the pediment is a marble relief, dated 1828, by E. H. Baily depicting *Britannia Acclaimed by Neptune.* Inside the portico is a long relief panel with seven roundels by J. E. Carew showing the *Progress of Navigation.* The original scheme for the entrance sculpture was British sea power and maritime trade. The two panels incorporated by Blore in the attic storey are by Richard Westmacott and were originally intended for the Marble Arch. They celebrate the Battle of Trafalgar (*The Death of Nelson*) and the Battle of Waterloo (*The Meeting of Blücher and Wellington*).

The Marble Arch was conceived by George IV and Nash as a celebration of victory in the Napoleonic Wars; hence the subject of these two panels.

The principal State Rooms of the palace are contained in the west range (behind the portico). The Queen's private apartments are in the north wing, and suites of rooms for important visitors occupy the main floor of the east wing, facing the Mall. Much of the ground floor of the palace is occupied by the offices of the Royal Household, and the kitchens are in the south wing.

THE GRAND HALL

The Grand Hall is of the same dimensions as the hall of the old Buckingham House and retains the same low proportions, stressing that this is the sub-storey with the main rooms above on a *piano nobile*, as in an Italian Renaissance palace. John Nash created dramatic spatial effects by lowering the floor of the central area. There are interesting vistas across the different levels into the adjoining spaces, and agreeable contrasts of light and shade. The spatial qualities of the room are enhanced by the use of rich materials. The floor and Corinthian columns are all of white Carrara marble, supplied by Joseph Browne who was sent to Italy by Nash to procure the marble used in the decoration of the palace. The Corinthian capitals are of gilded bronze supplied by Samuel Parker. The chimney-piece at the north end of the hall, facing the Grand Staircase, is among the finest in the palace and was supplied in 1829, at a cost of £1,000, by Joseph Theakston, 'the ablest carver of his time'. Its design shows the influence of Napoleon's architects Percier and Fontaine. At the top is a small bust of George IV, a comparatively modest 'signature' for the chief creator of Buckingham Palace. Originally the marmoreal quality of this hall was enhanced by the treatment of the walls, which were entirely lined with

SCULPTURE

1   Chimney-piece and overmantel by Joseph Theakston, 1829

2   Richard James Wyatt, *Nymph of Diana*, c.1850; completed by John Gibson and Benjamin Edward Spence after Wyatt's death

3   Wolf von Hoyer, *Psyche with a Lamp*, 1851

4   Pietro Tenerani, *Flora*, 1848

5   William Theed, *Psyche Lamenting the Loss of Cupid*, 1847

6   Pair of French polished granite urns with patinated and gilt bronze mounts, purchased by George IV in 1828 for Windsor Castle

FURNITURE

7   Set of hall chairs and settees made by Elward, Marsh & Tatham, mahogany painted with Prince of Wales feathers, 1802; made for the Hall at the Royal Pavilion, Brighton

8   Set of chairs, mahogany and gilt with tapering backs, painted with Queen Victoria's cypher, c.1790; made for the Hall at Carlton House, London

PORCELAIN

9   Set of four cisterns, Spode porcelain, with gilt bronze mounts, attributed to Benjamin Lewis Vulliamy, c.1820

RIGHT: The Grand Hall

coloured scagliola. The present white and gold decoration was executed in 1902 by C. H. Bessant for Edward VII.

The mahogany seat furniture, hall chairs and benches, was made for George IV when Prince of Wales and comes from two of his former residences, Brighton Pavilion and Carlton House. The latter stood at the other end of the Mall facing St James's Park and was the Prince's London home till he succeeded to the throne. The site is now occupied by Nash's Carlton House Terrace and the column commemorating the Duke of York. Carlton House was demolished when George IV decided to move to Buckingham Palace, but its magnificent fittings, furniture and works of art – the product of nearly forty years' discerning patronage on the part of the Prince – were all moved to Buckingham Palace and Windsor Castle. Throughout the State Rooms at Buckingham Palace, the visitor will notice magnificent chandeliers, French and English furniture, and paintings which George IV originally acquired for Carlton House and then moved to Buckingham Palace. The State Rooms were partly designed round his collection and were conceived as a magnificent setting for these superlative works of art.

THE GRAND STAIRCASE AND GUARD ROOM

The spatial complexity of the hall is continued in the Grand Staircase where Nash contrived an almost Baroque vista, the steps continuing in one straight flight from the half-landing as well as returning in two arms along the side. This plan was an ingenious arrangement to enable the State Rooms to be approached from two directions. It permitted both a circuit of all the State Rooms and an axial approach to the Throne Room. The staircase is on the site of George III's and the Duke of Buckingham's but is a complete rebuilding by Nash for George IV and is one of the principal architectural features of the palace.

The staircase provides a dramatic transition to the State Rooms on the first floor. Light floods down from the engraved glass skylights by Wainwright and Brothers, the patterns on which are reminiscent of white damask tablecloths.

The staircase itself is of Carrara marble, and the sumptuous gilt bronze balustrade embellished with rich Grecian foliage is reflected in the design of the plaster string-course round the walls. It was made by Samuel Parker in 1828–30 and is the finest of its type in England. It cost £3,900. Parker also provided the gilt metal mounts for the unique mahogany-framed mirror-plated doors designed by Nash and used throughout the State Rooms, adding enormously to their

BELOW LEFT: The Grand Staircase

BELOW: *State Ball at Buckingham Palace, 5 July 1848* by Eugène Lami. This watercolour shows Nash's Grand Staircase of the late 1820s with its balustrade by Samuel Parker and Grüner's polychrome wall decoration of 1845

glittery spaciousness. He charged 7d [nearly 3p] each for 'the little fleurs de lys' mouldings. The walls, which are now white and gold, were originally covered with polychrome panels of scagliola. The sculptural decorations in moulded plaster survive and were influenced by Percier and Fontaine's palace interiors for Napoleon. Here they were designed by the painter Thomas Stothard. The long rectangular reliefs of the four seasons were executed by his son Alfred Stothard, while the reliefs of cupids in the lunettes were modelled by Francis Bernasconi, the leading plasterer at the palace.

THE GRAND STAIRCASE

FITTINGS

1 Balustrade supplied by Samuel Parker, 1828–30, at a cost of £3,900

SCULPTURE

2 Jan Geefs, *Love and Malice*, 1859; birthday present from Queen Victoria to Prince Albert, 26 August 1859

3 Richard James Wyatt, *The Huntress*, 1850; birthday present from Queen Victoria to Prince Albert, 26 August 1850

4 Bronze 19th-century copy of Benvenuto Cellini's *Perseus and Medusa* in the Loggia dei Lanzi, Florence

PORCELAIN

5 Four Chinese porcelain vases with gilt bronze mounts, early 19th century; they may have been purchased by George IV from the dealer Robert Fogg in 1823 for £520

6 Two large Chinese *famille rose* baluster vases

PICTURES

Portraits of Queen Victoria's immediate ancestors and relations, illustrating her succession; an installation devised for Queen Victoria shortly after her Coronation in 1838

7 *William IV* by Sir Thomas Lawrence, 1827

8 *Prince George of Cumberland* (later George V, King of Hanover) by Sir Thomas Lawrence, 1828

9 *Princess Charlotte of Wales*, After George Dawe, c.1817

10 *Leopold I, King of the Belgians*, After George Dawe, 1844

11 *Queen Charlotte* by Sir William Beechey, 1796

12 *George III* by Sir William Beechey, 1799–1800

13 *Victoria, Duchess of Kent* by Sir George Hayter, 1835

14 *Augustus, Duke of Sussex* by Sir David Wilkie, 1833

15 *Edward, Duke of Kent* by George Dawe, 1818

16 *Queen Adelaide* by Sir Martin Archer Shee, 1836

THE GUARD ROOM

TAPESTRIES

17 Two Gobelins tapestries, 18th century; from the series *Les Portières des Dieux: Venus Symbolising Spring* (left); *Bacchus Symbolising Autumn* (right), and four *entrefenêtres*

SCULPTURE

18 John Gibson, *Queen Victoria*, 1847; originally partly tinted

19 Emil Wolff, *Prince Albert*, 1846; a replica of the original now at Osborne House, Isle of Wight. The Prince is dressed in Roman costume

20 Mary Thornycroft, *Princesses Victoria and Maud of Wales*, 1877

21 Benjamin Edward Spence, *Lady of the Lake*, 1861; birthday present from Queen Victoria to Prince Albert, 26 August 1861

22 Benjamin Edward Spence, *Highland Mary*, 1853; birthday present from Prince Albert to Queen Victoria, 24 May 1853

23 Mary Thornycroft, *Princess Louise of Wales*, 1877

FURNITURE

24 Set of seats by Morel & Seddon, 1826–8; made for Windsor Castle

25 Chandelier, probably supplied by Parker & Perry, c. 1811, for Carlton House, London

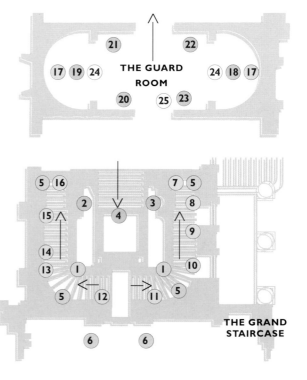

The approach to the Throne Room is of necessity much abridged from the traditional sequence in English palaces and comprises only the small Guard Room, the Drawing Room and the Throne Room itself. The Guard Room is more symbolic than useful. Though small, it is one of Nash's most successful spaces at the palace with its apsed ends, Carrara marble columns, and richly decorated plaster ceiling by Bernasconi. It forms an architectural overture to the glories to come. The white marble Neo-classical statues, including life-size portraits of herself and Prince Albert, were placed here by Queen Victoria. The glass chandelier, like those throughout the State Rooms, comes from Carlton House.

The three rooms extending along the courtyard side of the palace therefore form a shortened version of the traditional arrangement in English palaces, still to be seen at its full extent in the Wren State Rooms at Hampton Court Palace.

Because of lack of space at Buckingham Palace, the Guard Room is a mere formality and too small to accommodate the ceremonial guards on formal occasions. They are deployed instead in the adjoining rooms. The guards are composed of two corps. One is the Yeomen of the Guard – the royal bodyguard, initiated by Henry VII in 1485 – and the oldest bodyguard in the world; they still wear picturesque Tudor uniform. The other is the Gentlemen-at-Arms founded by Henry VIII in 1537, who wear magnificent scarlet and gold nineteenth-century-style uniforms with plumed helmets of polished steel.

BELOW: The Guard Room

THE GREEN DRAWING ROOM

The Green Drawing Room forms the ante-room to the Throne Room. Guests, official groups and delegations gather here before proceeding to the Throne Room or Music Room, where they are presented to the Sovereign. It occupies the site of the saloon in the old Buckingham House and Queen Charlotte's Saloon which had been redesigned by Sir William Chambers. It retains its former dimensions, rising through two storeys with a high coved ceiling, but was entirely remodelled by Nash for George IV. It keeps to a large extent the original character of the Nash architecture with green silk wall hangings framed by the plasterer George Jackson's lattice-patterned pilasters. The original silk (now replaced) was woven in Ireland at Queen Adelaide's request to provide employment there.

The ceiling is the first of a series of extraordinary designs by Nash with domes and concave and convex coving, which develops the tent-like 'Mogul' themes originally explored by him at the Royal Pavilion, Brighton; they are a unique feature of the State Rooms at Buckingham Palace. *Fraser's Magazine* in 1830 commented, 'It is indeed, not easy to conceive anything more splendid than the designs for ceilings which are to be finished in a style new in this country, partaking very much of the boldest style in the Italian taste of the fifteenth century ... they will present the effect of embossed gold ornaments.' The details and motifs are derived from a wide range of sources including the Italian Renaissance as well as Classical Greece and Rome; they stretch the canon of Georgian taste to the limits. The carved marble chimney-pieces are part of a series supplied for the palace by Joseph Browne at a cost of £6,000 between 1827 and 1830.

The State Rooms at Buckingham Palace were not completed at the

BELOW: Sèvres porcelain pot pourri vase, 1758, which probably belonged to Madame de Pompadour, Louis XV's mistress

THE GREEN DRAWING ROOM

LEFT: The Green Drawing
Room

PICTURES

1 *Augusta, Princess of Wales*, Studio of Allan Ramsay, *c.* 1764

2 *Frederick Henry, Charles Louis and Elizabeth* (children of Frederick V and Elizabeth, King and Queen of Bohemia), German School, *c.* 1620

3 *Edward Augustus, Duke of York* (brother of George III) by Nathaniel Dance, 1764

4 *James, Duke of Cambridge* (son of James II and his first wife Anne Hyde) by John Michael Wright, 1666–7

5 *Princesses Louisa Ann and Caroline Matilda* (later Queen of Denmark, both sisters of George III) by Francis Cotes, 1767

6 *Isabella Clara Eugenia and Catharina* (daughters of Philip II, King of Spain) by Sofonisba Anguissola (attrib.), *c.* 1569–70

7 *Richard, Marquess Wellesley* (brother of the 1st Duke of Wellington, when Lord Steward of the Household) by Sir Martin Archer Shee, *c.*1832

FURNITURE

8 Grand piano with six-octave action by Isaac Mott, 1817; purchased by George IV in 1820 for £238 5s it was placed in the Music Room Gallery at the Royal Pavilion, Brighton, together with the music stool

9 Four semi-circular pedestals, gilded wood, *c.* 1790; probably made in England to a French design for the Throne Room, Carlton House, London. They support gilt and patinated bronze French Empire candelabra

10 Suite of seat furniture by Morel & Seddon, 1826–8; made for Windsor Castle

11 Chest of drawers by Martin Carlin, ebony and gilt bronze, *c.* 1775. The raised *pietra dura* panels are about 100 years earlier in date; two have scratched on the back the name of Gian Ambrogio Giachetti who was employed by Louis XIV at the Gobelins manufactory to make mosaic panels. Bought by George IV in 1828, it had previously belonged to the singer Marie-Joséphine Laguerre

12 Regency centre table veneered in rosewood inlaid with brass

13 Four early 19th-century cut-glass chandeliers

14 Cabinet by Adam Weisweiler, veneered with Boulle marquetry with gilt bronze mounts, *c.* 1780–5. It is enriched with 17th-century panels of *pietra dura*; some, such as the two with single flowers, may have been made in Florence and those in relief at the Gobelins manufactory. Probably bought by George IV for Carlton House, London, in 1791

15 Pair of four-light candelabra by Benjamin Lewis Vulliamy, gilt and patinated bronze in the form of three female figures standing back to back, 1811; their design is inspired by the French Empire style

16 Two Flemish(?) cabinets, *c.* 1700, on later stands, veneered with tortoiseshell, pewter and ebony in *première-* and *contre-partie* marquetry (pewter in tortoiseshell and tortoiseshell in pewter)

17 French Empire clock with a figure of Apollo, probably designed by Martin-Eloi Lignereux with mounts supplied by Pierre-Philippe Thomire, 1803; bought by George IV in 1803

18 A pair of Empire gilt and patinated bronze seven light candelabra

PORCELAIN

19 Pot pourri vase, soft-paste Sèvres porcelain in the form of a ship, 1758; it probably belonged to Madame de Pompadour and was purchased by George IV in 1817

20 Vases. Sèvres porcelain with a green ground, second half of the 18th century

time of George IV's death in 1830. Their decoration and finishing was therefore carried on during the reign of William IV by Viscount Duncannon, the government minister responsible for Crown buildings. Duncannon was also in charge of finishing the new palace in 1834. As well as the contents of Carlton House, he brought some additional pieces from Windsor Castle. The gilt seat furniture in here is part of a huge set made by Morel & Seddon in 1826–8 for the Semi-State Rooms at Windsor Castle. The fluted pedestals for candelabra came from the Throne Room at Carlton House. This room now also contains two of George IV's finest purchases of French furniture, a cabinet by Adam Weisweiler and a chest of drawers by Martin Carlin, both embellished with superb seventeenth-century *pietra dura* panels. The magnificent Sèvres porcelain in here and throughout the State Rooms was also collected by George IV. Now divided between Buckingham Palace and Windsor Castle, it forms the finest group of Sèvres porcelain in the world, much of it of French royal provenance. During the French Revolution the contents of the palaces of France were systematically sold in order to raise much needed funds. Many of the finer pieces were bought by English collectors, led by George IV who as Prince of Wales and then as King employed a series of agents in Paris to acquire suitable objects, first for Carlton House and later for the new rooms at Windsor Castle and Buckingham Palace. Much of this incomparable collection remains in the settings for which he finally intended it. The Sèvres pot pourri vase here, for instance, was bought in Paris in 1817 by George IV's agent François Benois and cost the King 2,500 francs.

RIGHT: French chest of drawers by Martin Carlin, *c.* 1775. The *pietra dura* panels are about one hundred years earlier in date

THE THRONE ROOM

The Throne Room was intended for Investitures and ceremonial receptions of dignitaries by the Sovereign. It was also used by Queen Victoria, in the early years of her reign, as a ballroom. She was very fond of music and dancing and before the death of Prince Albert gave a whole series of concerts and balls at Buckingham Palace. Felix Mendelssohn played for her on three occasions. The Strauss orchestra was another favourite, and the Alice Polka, named after Queen Victoria's daughter Princess Alice, was first performed at a ball in the palace in 1849. Several of these occasions were *bals costumés*, such as the Stuart Ball held in the Throne Room in 1851, when all the guests dressed in the style of Charles II's court. The room proved too small, however, for most of its original purposes and was superseded by the new rooms in Pennethorne's south extension to the palace. The Throne Room is now used principally for the reception of formal addresses on important occasions, such as those presented at The Queen's Silver Jubilee in 1977. Royal wedding photographs are also usually taken in this room, including The Queen's own in 1947.

Twenty metres [60 feet] long, it is dominated by the almost Baroque 'proscenium' flanked by a pair of lively winged genii holding gilded garlands above the 'chairs of state'; the genii are Francis Bernasconi's masterpiece. They hold free-hanging swags modelled completely in the round — a virtuoso performance — from which is suspended a medallion with the cypher of George IV. The plaster frieze, designed by Thomas Stothard, is remarkable for its attempt to treat a medieval subject — the Wars of the Roses — as if it were the Parthenon frieze. It is only the Gothic armour that gives the game away. The subjects are the Battle of Tewkesbury (north), the Marriage of Henry VII and Elizabeth of York (east), the Battle of Bosworth (west) and Bellona, goddess of war, encouraging the troops (south). The same

BELOW: The wedding portrait of HRH Princess Elizabeth (now HM Queen Elizabeth II) and the Duke of Edinburgh, 20 November 1947

LEFT: The Throne Room

attempt to assimilate medieval ideas in Classical dress enlivens the bold display of heraldry of the four kingdoms of England, Scotland, Ireland and Hanover, and the Garter Stars, on the plaster cove. The elaborate door case opposite the throne is of scagliola (now painted) and was made by William Croggan; the little bust of William IV above shows that the decoration of this room was completed to the Nash designs after George IV's death. The crimson silk hangings on the walls are a recent restoration. The four carved and gilt trophies on either side of the throne may have come from Carlton House.

BELOW: The 'Oath of the Horatii' clock by Claude Galle, c. 1800

As in the other rooms, many of the contents came from Carlton House, including the bronze and cut-glass chandeliers, the gilt bronze candelabra on the chimney-piece and the velvet benches flanking the door from the Green Drawing Room. The most extraordinary items of Regency furniture are the two council chairs (flanking the throne dais) which were made for the Throne Room at Carlton House.

FITTINGS

1 Four trophies, gilded wood, c. 1795, said to have come from the Old Throne Room, Carlton House, London

FURNITURE

2 Oath of the Horatii clock by Claude Galle, c. 1800, based on the painting by Jacques-Louis David, 1784. Bought by George IV in 1809

3 Pair of candelabra attributed to Claude Galle, gilt and patinated bronze in the form of cornucopiae, early 19th century; purchased by George IV in 1814

4 Pair of council chairs by Tatham, Bailey & Sanders, 1812; supplied for George IV at Carlton House, London

5 Throne chairs of HM The Queen and the Duke of Edinburgh, by White, Allom & Co.; made for the Coronation ceremony of 1953

6 Throne chairs of King George VI and Queen Elizabeth by White, Allom & Co.; used during part of the Coronation ceremony of 1937

7 Throne chair of Queen Victoria by Thomas Dowbiggin, 1837

8 Chandeliers, cut glass and gilt bronze, c. 1810; probably from Carlton House, London

9 Pair of Regency giltwood and crimson velvet benches from the Ante-Throne Room at Carlton House

PORCELAIN

10 Pair of Chinese porcelain jardinières, early 18th century; the gilt bronze mounts are attributed to Benjamin Lewis Vulliamy, c. 1820

SCULPTURE

11 Carlo Marochetti, *Prince Arthur*, c. 1855

PICTURE

12 *Augusta, Duchess of Brunswick, with her Son Charles* (sister of George III and mother of Queen Caroline, consort of George IV) by Angelica Kauffmann, 1767

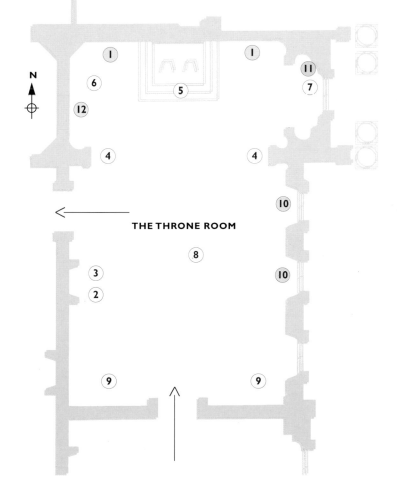

THE THRONE ROOM

THE PICTURE GALLERY

This is the great spine of the State Apartments. It is 50 metres [155 feet] long and is entirely top lit. It occupies the site of the first-floor rooms of old Buckingham House. It was designed by Nash to display George IV's outstanding collection of Dutch and Flemish paintings, many of which still hang here. At Carlton House, paintings and sculpture had been scattered throughout the rooms, but for Buckingham Palace George IV planned a sculpture gallery and a picture gallery

(one over the other) specially for the display of his finest works of art. The original ceiling was a complex design combining a timber hammerbeam frame with hanging pendants and a series of 17 little glazed saucer domes or lanterns. It was something of a practical failure as it leaked and failed to throw light on the pictures. It was modified by Blore and totally remodelled for King George V in 1914 as a glazed segmental arched ceiling. The door cases were also simplified and the columnar screen at the south end was redesigned. The architect for these changes was Frank Baines, chief architect of the Office of Works. The wood carvings, in the style of Grinling Gibbons, were made by H. H. Martyn of Cheltenham. The result is rather like the interior of the saloon of one of the great ocean liners of this period. Its 'subdued tastefulness' makes a striking contrast to the extreme

opulence of Nash's adjoining rooms. The walls were hung in 1914 with olive-green silk damask woven by Warners, but this has since been replaced by the present pink flock coverings.

The four Carrara marble chimney-pieces supplied by Joseph Browne in the 1820s survive from the gallery's first incarnation and were designed by Nash. They each display a circular portrait relief of a famous artist: Dürer, Rubens, Titian and Michelangelo. In the mid-nineteenth century there were 185 paintings in the gallery. Today it is the quality of the paintings that makes this room so remarkable: the collection includes works by Rubens and Rembrandt, Van Dyck and Vermeer.

The Royal Collection is today the most extensive private collection in the world. It was begun by Charles I in the seventeenth century. Though his works of art were dispersed during the Commonwealth, several were later re-acquired, notably his magnificent equestrian portrait with Monsieur de St Antoine painted by Van Dyck in 1633. The collection was considerably enriched in the eighteenth century by Frederick, Prince of Wales (the eldest son of George II), and by George III. The largest group of paintings in the Picture Gallery, however, is that assembled by George IV. These include the wonderful landscapes by Cuyp, *The Farm at Laeken* by Rubens and also the Rembrandt portraits *Agatha Bas* and *The Ship Builder and his Wife*.

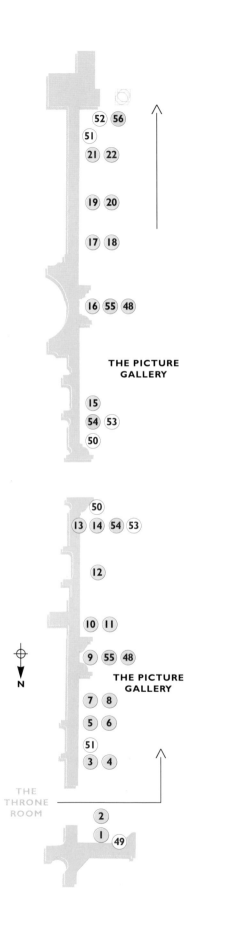

THE PICTURE GALLERY

THE PICTURE GALLERY

N

THE
THRONE
ROOM

The arrangement of pictures has changed over the years. Most of the paintings now in the Picture Gallery were acquired by Charles I; Frederick, Prince of Wales; George III or, principally, George IV. Outstanding works are marked with an asterisk.

1   *The Libyan Sibyl* by Guercino, c. 1651*

2   *A Family Group* by Barent Graat, 1658

3   *The Stolen Kiss* by David Teniers the Younger, c. 1640

4   *Interior of a Tavern with Cardplayers and a Violin Player* by Jan Steen, c. 1665

5   *Virgin and Child* by Sir Anthony van Dyck, c. 1630–2

6   *The Passage Boat* by Aelbert Cuyp, c. 1650*

7   *A Mountainous Landscape with Herdsmen Driving Cattle down a Road* by Nicholas Berchem, 1673

8   *A Lady at the Virginals with a Gentleman ('The Music Lesson')* by Johannes Vermeer, c. 1670*

9   *Landscape with Two Young Children Offering Fruit to a Woman* by Francesco Zuccarelli, c. 1743

10   *Fishermen on the Seashore* by David Teniers the Younger, c. 1660

11   *Portrait of a Man* by Frans Hals, c. 1630*

12   *The Ship Builder and his Wife* by Rembrandt van Rijn, c. 1633*

13   *Cows in a Pasture beside a River before the Ruins of the Abbey of Rijnsburg* by Aelbert Cuyp, 1640–50

14   *Agatha Bas* by Rembrandt van Rijn, 1641*

15   *Charles I and Henrietta Maria with their Two Eldest Children ('The Greate Peece')* by Sir Anthony van Dyck, 1632*

16   *Venice: The Piazzetta towards the Torre dell'Orologio* by Antonio Canaletto, c. 1728*

17   *A Caprice Landscape with a Fountain and an Artist Sketching* by Luca Carlevaris, c. 1710

18   *Seascape with Jonah and the Whale* by Gaspard Dughet, c. 1653

19   *Birds and a Spaniel* by Melchior de Hondecoeter, c. 1665

20   *Landscape with St George and the Dragon* by Sir Peter Paul Rubens, c. 1630*

21   *A Caprice View of a Seaport* by Luca Carlevaris, c. 1710

22   *The Rape of Europa* by Claude Lorrain, 1667*

48   Chimney-pieces supplied by Joseph Browne and carved by Italian sculptors, late 1820s; they incorporate profile busts of Titian, Rubens, Dürer and Michelangelo

FURNITURE

49   Pair of cabinets by Pierre Garnier, veneered with ebony and inlaid with panels of pewter, tortoiseshell and brass, c. 1770; bought for George IV in Paris in 1819

50   Four armchairs by Georges Jacob, c. 1786; imported into England by Dominique Daguerre in the late

1780s, they were placed in the Prince's bedroom at Carlton House, London

51   Set of four French console tables attributed to Adam Weisweiler, marble-topped and veneered with tulipwood, c. 1785; the gilt bronze scrollwork was added by Benjamin Vulliamy in 1811

52   Two pedestals supplied by Gilles Joubert, veneered with trellis marquetry in kingwood and tulipwood, 1762. Made to support clocks giving solar and lunar time, they originally stood on either side of the alcove in Louis XV's bedroom at Versailles. They now support 18th-century bronze

PICTURES (right wall)

23 *The Death of Cleopatra* by Guido Reni, *c.* 1628

24 *Family of Jan-Baptista Anthoine* by Gonzales Coques, copper, 1664

25 *The Listening Housewife* by Nicolaes Maes, 1655

26 *The Cello Player* by Gabriel Metsu, *c.* 1665

27 *The Hayfield* by Philips Wouwermans, *c.* 1660

28 *The Assumption of the Virgin* by Sir Peter Paul Rubens, panel, *c.* 1611*

29 *The Mystic Marriage of St Catherine* by Sir Anthony van Dyck, *c.* 1630*

30 *Milkmaids with Cattle in a Landscape ('The Farm at Laeken')* by Sir Peter Paul Rubens, panel, *c.* 1617–18*

31 *A Horse Fair in front of a Town* by Philips Wouwermans, *c.* 1660

32 *A Courtyard in Delft at Evening: A Woman Spinning* by Pieter de Hooch, *c.* 1656*

33 *Landscape with Two Seated Women Embracing* by Francesco Zuccarelli, *c.* 1743

34 *Vincenzo Avogadro* by Domenico Fetti, *c.* 1620

35 *A Calm: A States Yacht under Sail, close to the Shore, and Many Other Vessels* by Willem van de Velde the Younger, panel, *c.* 1655*

36 *Christ Healing the Paralytic* by Sir Anthony van Dyck, *c.* 1619

37 *Peasants Dancing outside a Country House* by David Teniers the Younger, panel, 1645

38 *Zeger van Hontsum* by Sir Anthony van Dyck, *c.* 1630

39 *'The Golden Leeuw' at Sea in Heavy Weather* by Willem van de Velde the Younger, *c.* 1671

40 *Charles I with M. de St Antoine* by Sir Anthony van Dyck, 1633*

41 *Venice: Piazza S. Marco from a Corner of the Basilica* by Antonio Canaletto, 1728*

42 *A Caprice View with a Shipyard* by Luca Carlevaris, *c.* 1710

43 *Landscape with a Waterfall* by Gaspard Poussin, *c.* 1653–4

44 *A Village Revel* by Jan Steen, *c.* 1673

45 *Landscape with a Negro Page* by Aelbert Cuyp, *c.* 1655*

46 *A Caprice View of a Harbour* by Luca Carlevaris, *c.* 1710

47 *Landscape with Figures by a Pool* by Gaspard Poussin, *c.* 1665

busts of the Emperors Augustus and Vespasian. Acquired by George IV in 1818

53 Two pairs of Boulle cabinets in brass and pewter with gilt bronze figurative plaques and friezes, acquired in 1828

Giltwood sofas, probably those supplied by William Adair in 1799 for Queen Charlotte's saloon in Buckingham House

PORCELAIN AND LACQUER

54 Japanese lacquer bowls with French gilt bronze mounts in the Louis XV and Louis XVI styles, 18th century

55 Two pairs of vases, hard-paste Sèvres porcelain painted in platinum and gold on a black ground with chinoiserie scenes and with gilt bronze mounts, *c.* 1790–2; and another pair, with an undecorated black ground and siren mounts, *c.* 1786

56 Pair of large celadon vases in the form of ewers with French gilt bronze mounts, early 19th century

57 Pair of *lac burgauté* vases, with gilt bronze mounts, by the Vulliamys, early 19th century

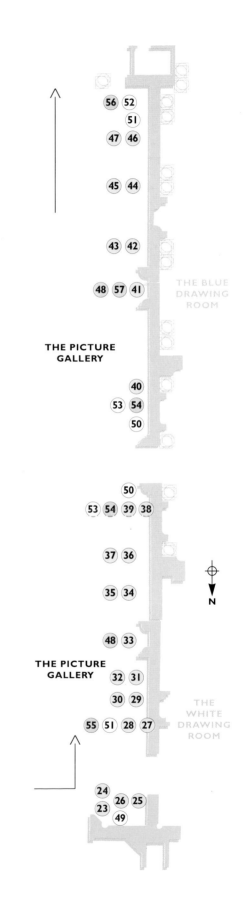

THE BLUE DRAWING ROOM

THE PICTURE GALLERY

N

THE PICTURE GALLERY

THE WHITE DRAWING ROOM

RIGHT: One of two pedestals by Gilles Joubert, made in 1762, originally intended to support clocks giving solar and lunar time. They now support 18th-century bronze busts of the Emperors Augustus (shown here) and Vespasian

ABOVE: *The Ship Builder and his Wife* by Rembrandt van Rijn, c. 1633

LEFT: *Milkmaids with Cattle in a Landscape ('The Farm at Laeken')* by Sir Peter Paul Rubens, c. 1617–18

ABOVE: *A Lady at the Virginals with a Gentleman* by Johannes Vermeer, c. 1670

LEFT: *Venice: The Piazzetta towards the Torre dell'Orologio* by Antonio Canaletto, *c.* 1728

RIGHT: *A Courtyard in Delft at Evening: A Woman Spinning* by Pieter de Hooch, *c.* 1656

RIGHT: *Charles I and Henrietta Maria with their Two Eldest Children* by Sir Anthony Van Dyck, 1632

BELOW: *The Death of Cleopatra* by Guido Reni, *c.* 1628

THE PICTURE GALLERY LOBBY

The Picture Gallery Lobby is divided from the main part of the gallery by a screen of white marble Corinthian columns, but is otherwise treated in the same architectural manner, with a door case by Martyn of Cheltenham and a plaster frieze of 1914 by Frank Baines. The most interesting object here is the life-size marble statue by Sir Francis Chantrey of Mrs Jordan and two of her children. Mrs Jordan was a celebrated actress and the mistress of the Duke of Clarence, later William IV, before his marriage to Princess Adelaide of Saxe-Meiningen and his succession to the throne. Mrs Jordan had five sons and five daughters by the Duke. They took the name Fitzclarence and the eldest son, George Augustus Frederick, was created Earl of Munster in 1831. This charming statue was commissioned by William IV in 1834, after Mrs Jordan's death. It was bequeathed to The Queen in 1975 by the 5th and last Earl of Munster.

Hanging behind the statue is one of George IV's more unusual acquisitions, a large embroidered silk religious hanging depicting the Annunciation. It dates from the mid-seventeenth century and was originally made for an Italian church, where such needlework panels were hung on great feast days.

ABOVE: Marble statue of Mrs Jordan and two of her children by Sir Francis Chantrey, 1834

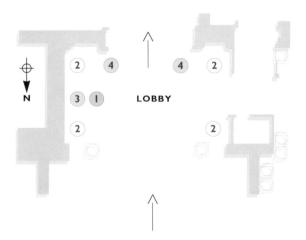

N

LOBBY

SCULPTURE

1   Sir Francis Chantrey, *Mrs Jordan and Two Children*, 1834; commissioned by William IV after her death. The group was bequeathed to HM The Queen by the Earl of Munster in 1975

FURNITURE

2   Set of lyre-backed chairs, part gilded, probably made for Carlton House by François Hervé, c. 1790

EMBROIDERY

3   Large Italian needlework panel, representing the Annunciation within an arabesque border, mid-17th century

PORCELAIN

4   Pair of large octagonal Chinese porcelain vases, late 18th century

THE SILK TAPESTRY ROOM

RIGHT: *Queen Charlotte with her Two Eldest Sons* by Allan Ramsay, *c.* 1764

This indeterminate space was contrived by Blore as a link between the Grand Staircase, the Picture Gallery and the garden-front State Rooms. It takes its name from the Italian needlework panels which formerly hung in this area. The room is notable for its contents. The large *River Landscape with the Finding of Moses* by Francesco Zuccarelli is one of a number of paintings commissioned by George III directly from the artist. It is signed 'Francesco Zuccarelli, London 1768'. Zuccarelli was an Italian artist who settled in London in the mid-eighteenth century and a founder member of the Royal Academy. His work was much admired by George III, who acquired thirty of his landscapes. The monumental French pedestal clock with Rococo ormolu decoration was another of George IV's acquisitions for Carlton House, where it formed a focal point on the principal staircase.

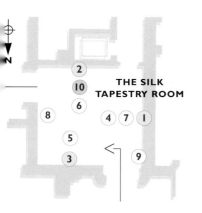

THE SILK TAPESTRY ROOM

PICTURES

1 *River Landscape with the Finding of Moses* by Francesco Zuccarelli, 1768

2 *Queen Charlotte with her Two Eldest Sons* by Allan Ramsay, *c.* 1764

3 *The Mock Election* by Benjamin Robert Haydon, 1827

FURNITURE

4 Chest of drawers by Adam Weisweiler, mahogany veneered, late 18th century

5 Table by Morel & Seddon, ebony with *pietra dura* slab and gilt bronze mounts, raised on four pairs of gilded wood supports, *c.* 1828; made for Windsor Castle

6 Side table by Adam Weisweiler, veneered with ebony, *c.* 1785; the panels of *pietra dura* probably date from the late 17th century. It was bought in Paris for George IV in 1816

7 French clock by François-Louis Godon, white marble and gilt bronze, carved with figures of Venus and Cupid, 1792

8 Monumental pedestal clock, veneered with tulipwood and fitted with elaborately chased gilt and patinated bronze mounts. Although stamped by Duhamel (active 1750–1801) it was probably made in the 1730s, possibly by Jean-Pierre Latz. Bought by George IV in 1816, it was placed at the foot of the staircase in Carlton House, London

9 Pair of marble vases with gilt bronze tripods and mounts; French, late 18th century. Possibly supplied by Dominique Daguerre for Carlton House in the late 1780s

SCULPTURE

10 Bronze reduction of the equestrian statue of Louis XV after Edmé Bouchardon which was unveiled in 1763 in the Place Louis XV (now Place de la Concorde), Paris; this reduction is one of seven cast by Louis-Claude Vassé, *c.* 1764

THE EAST GALLERY

Queen Victoria found George IV's State Rooms, despite their magnificence, too small for court entertainments and ceremonial. She and Prince Albert therefore added a large new block to the south end of the west range of the palace in 1853–5 to provide extra space including a vast new ballroom and a series of galleries for royal processions. These rooms were designed by James Pennethorne, who had been a protégé of Nash at the Office of Works; they were built by William Cubitt. Their interior

LEFT: *The Coronation of Queen Victoria* by Sir George Hayter, 1838

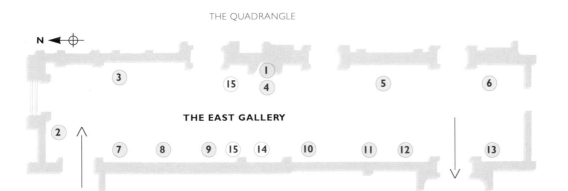

THE QUADRANGLE

N

THE EAST GALLERY

FITTINGS

1 Chimney-piece supplied by Joseph Browne, late 1820s, incorporating a profile bust of Rembrandt

PICTURES

2 *Mrs Jordan as the Comic Muse* by John Hoppner, 1786

3 *The Family of Balthasar Gerbier*, Studio of Sir Peter Paul Rubens, c.1630

4 *George, Prince of Wales* (later George IV) by John Russell, 1791; the Prince is in the uniform of the Royal Kentish Bowmen

5 *The Family of Queen Victoria* by Franz Xaver Winterhalter, 1846

6 *Frederick, Duke of York* by Sir Joshua Reynolds, 1788

7 *Queen Charlotte* by Benjamin West, 1782

8 *Prince Adolphus (later Duke of Cambridge), with Princesses Mary and Sophia* by Benjamin West, 1778

9 *George III* by Benjamin West, 1779

10 *Francis, 5th Duke of Bedford* by John Hoppner, c. 1797

11 *The Coronation of Queen Victoria* by Sir George Hayter, 1838

12 *Francis, 5th Earl of Moira and 1st Marquess of Hastings* by John Hoppner, c. 1793

13 *Caroline, Princess of Wales, and Princess Charlotte* by Sir Thomas Lawrence, c. 1806

FURNITURE

14 Large clock signed by the Parisian bronze manufacturer De La Croix, gilt and patinated bronze, c. 1775; the dial is a later insertion by Vulliamy. The pedestal incorporates four gilt bronze plaques of 16th-century design

15 Two pairs of candelabra by Pierre-Philippe Thomire, gilt bronze supported by figures of patinated bronze, c. 1810; they entered the collection in 1813. They stand on ebony and brass pedestals, French, early 19th century

finishing and decoration was executed under the immediate direction of the Prince Consort and the team of artists whom he admired. These included Professor Ludwig Grüner from Dresden and the artist Nicolà Consoni from Rome, where the latter had been responsible for some of the paintings in the basilica of St Paul's outside the Walls. Much of this decoration has been covered up in the course of various redecorations in this century, but Consoni's gold and grisaille panels of cupids at play survive round the top of the East Gallery.

The East Gallery extends southwards towards the Ballroom from the Grand Staircase and contains one of the marble chimneypieces designed by Nash and made under Joseph Browne's direction at Carrara in the 1820s, *en suite* with those in the Picture Gallery. It contains a carved portrait roundel of Rembrandt.

BELOW: The East Gallery

THE CROSS AND WEST GALLERIES

The Cross and the West Galleries are smaller than the East Gallery but were also designed by Pennethorne and decorated originally by Ludwig Grüner. The West Gallery is the most successful as an architectural space with its fine proportions and semi-circular ceiling. The *tympana* at either end have spirited plaster sculptures in the style of those in George IV's rooms. These are the work of William Theed the Younger, a sculptor who was admired by Prince Albert. The Prince's aim was to introduce a

LEFT: *Sancho Panza Despairs at the Loss of his Donkey*; one of four tapestries from a series of twenty-eight illustrating the exploits of Don Quixote, Gobelins, second half of the 18th century, given to George IV by the artist Richard Cosway

serious 'artistic' note into the decoration of the palace as a demon-stration of the High Renaissance, Raphaelesque style that he and Grüner were trying to promote in England. It is similar to that favoured by other German princely patrons of the mid-nineteenth century, as can be seen at Potsdam, Dresden and Munich.

These spaces are now used to display works of art from the Royal Collection. In the West Gallery are four Gobelins tapestries from the *Don Quixote* series which were given to George IV in 1789 by the artist Richard Cosway, one of the 'Carlton House set'. Cosway himself had been given them, while in Paris two years earlier, by Louis XVI. Cosway was one of the Prince's chief artistic advisers in the 1780s and helped to influence George IV's taste for French fashion and art, with the results which are so spectacularly represented at Buckingham Palace.

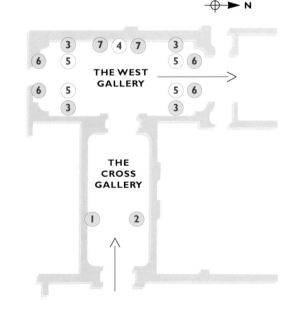

THE CROSS GALLERY

PICTURES

1 *Christianborg Palace from Højbro Plads, Copenhagen* by Heinrich Hansen, 1863

2 *Bernstorff House and Park* by Frederik Kiaerskou, 1863

THE WEST GALLERY

TAPESTRIES

3 Four tapestries woven at the Gobelins manufactory from a series of 28 illustrating the exploits of Don Quixote, second half of the 18th century; given to George IV by the artist Richard Cosway

FURNITURE

4 Boulle knee-hole desk, veneered with tortoiseshell, ebony and brass, late 17th century

5 Giltwood chairs designed by Robert Jones and made by Tatham, Bailey & Sanders for the Royal Pavilion, Brighton, 1823

PORCELAIN

6 Four Chinese porcelain vases on marble pedestals with mounts by the Vulliamys, 1808–14

7 Two Chinese Imari-pattern square baluster vases and covers *c.* 1750

THE STATE DINING ROOM

LEFT: The State Dining Room

The State Dining Room was originally intended to be a music room; the pair of white marble chimney-pieces, possibly the work of Matthew Cotes Wyatt, show flanking female figures playing musical instruments. It is possible that the bed of the ceiling with its three little saucer domes may also have been designed by Nash as it is more refined than the coving of Blore's surround with its heavy and relentless bracketing.

The room was completed as a dining room for William IV and for Queen Victoria, both of whose cyphers can be found in the plaster roundels in the penetration of the coving. The conversion of this room to a dining room was one of William IV's few alterations to his predecessors' layout of the State Rooms. The new King wanted a dining room on the principal floor adjoining the drawing rooms, rather than on the ground floor as Nash and George IV had envisaged. The character of the room, with its somewhat coarse and heavy detailing, is now largely due to Edward Blore, who was commissioned by the Government to finish the palace after George IV's death and Nash's dismissal for financial incompetence.

BELOW: *King George IV in Garter Robes* by Sir Thomas Lawrence and studio, *c.* 1820

Blore had a reputation for being able to work within a budget. The pier glasses, pelmets and other florid gilded enrichments of the room were designed by him.

The principal feature of the room is the series of splendid, full-length royal portraits. These were placed here by Queen Victoria, who had a particular interest in portraits of her family and arranged several of the rooms as dynastic galleries. Those in here are the State Portraits of all the Hanoverian sovereigns of Britain. Their gilded frames were supplied by Ponsonby & Sons in 1840. The alcove at the south end, which now contains the entrance to the West Gallery, was originally the sideboard recess, used for displaying gold plate during banquets, but it was altered when Pennethorne's wing was added in 1853–5.

The State Dining Room is used regularly by The Queen for official entertaining, luncheons and formal dinners. On these occasions the tables are set with part of the great silver-gilt services acquired over many years by George IV, mainly from the Crown goldsmiths Rundell, Bridge & Rundell. Some examples are displayed in this room, including the pair of ewers and stands made for the King in 1822 and an oval tureen by Paul Storr. George IV had a particular love of gold plate, and commissioned some of the most magnificent pieces ever made in England.

A great feature of the State Dining Room and all the rooms on the west side of the palace is the beautiful views over the gardens landscaped in the

ABOVE: One of a pair of silver-gilt-ewers and stands by Rundell, Bridge & Rundell, 1822

BELOW: The Queen addressing Asian and European leaders at a dinner, April 1998. Seated on The Queen's right is The Sultan of Brunei and on her left Germany's then Chancellor, Dr Helmut Kohl

THE STATE DINING ROOM

RIGHT: The 'Apollo clock', by
Pierre-Philippe Thomire

1820s for George IV by Nash and William Townsend Aiton, the head gardener at Kew. The lake and the picturesque, naturalistic planting of trees and shrubs, and the green lawns, make the palace truly *rus in urbe*. The gardens form the setting for the summer Garden Parties, started by Queen Victoria and originally called 'breakfasts' despite taking place in the afternoon; they were revived by King George VI. These have become an increasingly popular feature of the Buckingham Palace year.

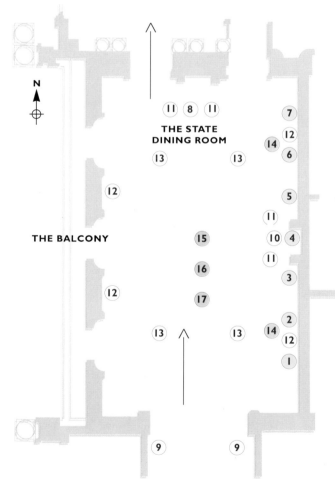

PICTURES

The display illustrates the development of state portraiture during the second half of the 18th century.

1   *Caroline, Princess of Wales* (later Queen, wife of George II) by Sir Godfrey Kneller, 1716

2   *Frederick, Prince of Wales* by Jean-Baptiste van Loo, 1742

3   *Queen Charlotte* (wife of George III) by Allan Ramsay, c. 1763

4   *King George IV in Garter Robes*, Studio of Sir Thomas Lawrence, c. 1820

5   *George III* by Allan Ramsay, c. 1763

6   *Augusta, Princess of Wales* (wife of Frederick, Prince of Wales) by Jean-Baptiste van Loo, 1742

7   *George II*, Studio of John Shackleton, 1755–7

FURNITURE

8   Clock by Pierre-Philippe Thomire, gilt bronze and marble, representing Apollo in his chariot drawn by four horses, early 19th century; bought by George IV in 1810, its movement was changed by Benjamin Lewis Vulliamy in 1834

9   Pair of candelabra by Thomire & Cie, malachite and gilt bronze, c. 1828, on Regency giltwood tripods carved with griffins

10   Clock by Benjamin Lewis Vulliamy, marble and gilt bronze, fitted with three porcelain figures by William Duesbury of Derby, 1788; designed for the Prince of Wales (later George IV)

11   Set of four five-light candelabra by François Rémond, gilt bronze on red marble bases, 1783; made for the closet decorated in the Turkish manner in the comte d'Artois' apartments at Versailles. Bought by George IV in 1820

12   Set of parcel gilt mahogany sideboards with gilt bronze and mirrored glass backs, 1838

13   Four early 19th-century English cut-glass and gilt bronze chandeliers

PORCELAIN

14   Chinese celadon porcelain vases with French and English gilt bronze mounts, 18th and early 19th century; most of these were at the Royal Pavilion, Brighton, in the early 19th century

TABLE SILVER

15   Oval tureen, cover and stand by Paul Storr, silver gilt, 1812; made for George IV

16   Pair of wine bottle coolers by Digby Scott and Benjamin Smith, silver gilt, 1803; made for George IV

17   Pair of ewers and stands by Rundell, Bridge & Rundell, silver gilt, 1822; made for George IV

N

THE STATE
DINING ROOM

THE BALCONY

THE BLUE DRAWING ROOM

LEFT: The Blue Drawing
Room

George IV intended this as a ballroom though it has been superseded in that function by Queen Victoria's larger Ballroom in the south-west wing. Guests gather here for drinks before large luncheon parties and grand state and diplomatic occasions. This is one of the finest rooms in the palace and the *ne plus ultra* of Georgian sumptuousness in decoration, even more splendid than the Throne Room sequence on the east front. It is 21 metres [68 feet] long and divided into bays by giant Corinthian columns. It was first called the South Drawing Room and its original decoration was a symphony of red with porphyry scagliola columns, crimson velvet curtains and figured silk wall hangings. It now has a blue flock paper installed by Queen Mary near the beginning of the twentieth century, while the Corinthian columns were painted to resemble onyx, covering up defects in the scagliola, in the reign of Queen Victoria. The ceiling with its great billowing coves and bold console brackets shows Nash at his most daring and original.

The three moulded plaster reliefs in the *tympana* are by William Pitts (1835) and have a literary theme depicting the Apotheoses of Shakespeare (north), of Spenser (south) and of Milton (facing north).

ABOVE: Sèvres porcelain vase
(*vase royal*), c. 1770

FAR LEFT: *State Portrait of King
George V* by Sir Samuel Luke
Fildes, 1911–12

LEFT: *State Portrait of Queen
Mary* by Sir William Llewellyn,
1911–13

ABOVE: Queen Elizabeth
(now Queen Elizabeth The
Queen Mother)
photographed in the Blue
Drawing Room by Cecil
Beaton, 1939

William Pitts (1790–1840) designed and modelled most of the high relief plasterwork in the State Rooms. He started life as a silver chaser and modeller and executed the famous silver-gilt *Achilles Shield* to Flaxman's design. His work at Buckingham Palace has considerable grace and charm but is perhaps too small in scale to be appreciated in its lofty situation. The florid whiteness of the forms and foliage stands out against a richly gilded ground. This and the following two rooms are the principal features of Buckingham Palace. The richness of their fittings and fixtures distinguishes them from any comparable State Rooms in England, while the originality of their architecture marks them out from contemporary palace rooms on the Continent. The aim of George IV and Nash, in which they triumphantly succeeded, was to create an aura of extreme opulence.

Only the architectural part of the room was completed by the time of George IV's death, and the decoration and the furnishing were carried out in the reign of William IV under the supervision of Viscount Duncannon. The gilt sofas and some of the armchairs were made for Carlton House in the early part of the nineteenth century. The four marble side tables with gilt bronze mounts are the work of Alexandre-Louis Bellangé (*c.* 1823) and were acquired for Windsor Castle by George IV in 1825. They were brought here in 1834 by Lord Duncannon as part of the furnishing and fitting up of the new Buckingham Palace State Rooms for William IV. They had to be adapted slightly to fit into the spaces between the plinths of the Corinthian columns. The cut-glass chandeliers are from the Crimson Drawing Room at Carlton House.

In this room is one of George IV's favourite possessions – the Table of the Grand Commanders. The top is of Sèvres porcelain painted in *trompe l'oeil* to resemble sardonyx with the head of Alexander the Great surrounded by similar cameo-like portraits – heads of twelve other great commanders of Antiquity. It was commissioned by Napoleon in 1806 when, as the conqueror of all

BELOW: The Table of the Grand Commanders, 1806–12, a gift from Louis XVIII to George IV in 1817

46

THE BLUE DRAWING ROOM

Europe and the recently crowned Emperor of the French, he was at his apogee and saw himself as a modern Alexander the Great. The painting is by Louis-Bertin Parant and the ormolu mounts by Pierre-Philippe Thomire. It was presented by Louis XVIII of France to George IV, when still Prince Regent, in 1817. George IV was so thrilled by this magnificent trophy that he instructed the painter Sir Thomas Lawrence to include it in his State Portraits. It was placed in the Bow Drawing Room at Carlton House before being brought here.

Other Sèvres vases from George IV's incomparable collection can be seen in this room, notably the garnitures of dark blue vases — many of rare and unusual shape — on the chimney-pieces and Bellangé side tables.

ABOVE: Astronomical clock, c. 1790 by Jean-Antoine Lépine

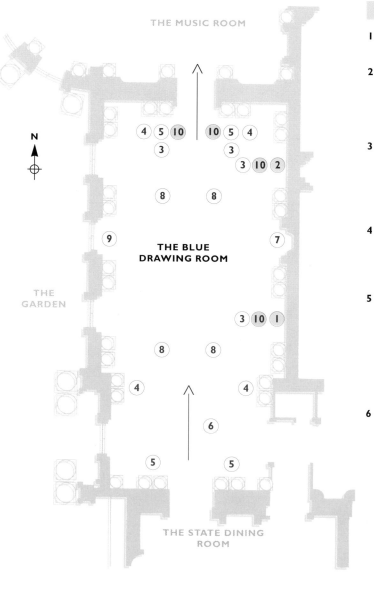

PICTURES

1 *George V* by Sir Samuel Luke Fildes, 1911–12

2 *Queen Mary* by Sir William Llewellyn, 1911–13

FURNITURE

3 Set of four side tables by Alexandre-Louis Bellangé, marble and gilt bronze, c. 1823; bought by George IV in 1825 for Windsor Castle

4 Parts of four sets of settees and armchairs by Tatham, Bailey & Sanders, and other makers, c. 1810–28

5 Two pairs of candelabra attributed to François Rémond, gilt bronze, c. 1787; probably acquired by George IV for Carlton House, London, in the 1780s. There are two further pairs in the Music Room

6 'Table of the Grand Commanders', hard-paste Sèvres porcelain with gilt bronze mounts, 1806–12. The table-top is painted by Louis-Bertin Parant with the head of Alexander the Great (centre) surrounded by the heads of 12 other commanders from Antiquity, all in imitation of cameo reliefs. The mounts are by Pierre-Philippe Thomire. Commissioned by Napoleon in 1806, it was presented to George IV by Louis XVIII in 1817

7 Astronomical clock with three dials by Jean-Antoine Lépine, marble and gilt bronze, c. 1790, bought by George IV in 1790

8 Set of four cut-glass chandeliers, English, c. 1810

9 Giltwood centre table with a late 17th-century Italian *pietra dura* top

PORCELAIN

10 Vases, Sèvres porcelain painted with a dark blue ground, second half of the 18th century; they include some rare models of ambitious design

THE MUSIC ROOM

LEFT: The Music Room

Originally known as the Bow Drawing Room, this occupies the centre of the garden front behind the semi-circular bow window – an architectural feature much admired by George IV, who liked rooms with a bow on one side. It is more disciplined than the Blue Drawing Room, with an ingeniously designed vaulted and domed ceiling, lavishly gilded. The diagonal coffering of the dome is moulded with the rose, thistle and shamrock, emblematic of the three kingdoms of England, Scotland and Ireland. This room is entirely Nash's design as it was completed in 1831 and has not been altered since. This is the room where guests, having assembled in the Green Drawing Room, are presented before a dinner or a banquet. Here too, royal babies are sometimes christened. The Queen's three eldest children were all baptised here in water brought from the River Jordan.

BELOW: *The Music Room* by Douglas Morison, 1843

THE MUSIC ROOM

A spectacular feature of the room is the parquet floor of satinwood, rosewood, tulipwood, mahogany, holly and other woods. It was made by Thomas Seddon and cost £2,400. It is a triumph of English craftsmanship and one of the finest of its type in the country. The columns round the wall are of lapis lazuli scagliola; and originally the walls were hung with bright yellow silk, which must have presented a dramatic visual impact in conjunction with the blue columns. In the *tympana* at the tops of the walls are three graceful reliefs by William Pitts depicting the Progress of Rhetoric. The subjects are Harmony (north), Eloquence (east) and Pleasure (south). Over the white marble fireplaces are large arched mirrors in concave plaster frames designed by Nash which complete the architectural treatment of the room.

The carved and gilt Louis XVI seat furniture was acquired by George IV and comes from Carlton House. This set was supplied from Paris by Georges Jacob, through the dealer Dominique Daguerre, for Henry Holland's interior there in the late 1780s. The spectacular chandeliers, of gilt bronze and cut glass, also come from Carlton House and are among the most beautiful in the palace. The Carlton House chandeliers were considered at the time of their manufacture to be the finest in Europe. The windows in the bow, like all the windows on the principal floor of Buckingham Palace, have large-paned glass casements, rather than small-paned Georgian sashes. They were a technological innovation in the 1820s and are one of the earliest surviving English uses of plate glass. They enhance the views out over the surrounding gardens and parks.

FITTINGS

1   Marquetry floor, satinwood, holly and other woods inlaid with the cypher of George IV, 1831; it cost £2,400

FURNITURE

2   Throne chairs of King George V and Queen Mary, when Prince and Princess of Wales, used during the Coronation of Edward VII in 1902

3   Small armchairs and settees by Georges Jacob, c. 1786; imported into England by Dominique Daguerre in the late 1780s for Carlton House, London

4   Boudoir grand piano by John Broadwood & Sons, 20th century

5   Vase by Pierre-Philippe Thomire, patinated and gilt bronze, early 19th century; bought by George IV in 1812

6   Pair of English chandeliers, cut glass and gilt bronze, early 19th century

PORCELAIN

7   Vases, soft-paste Sèvres porcelain; those on the left-hand chimney-piece supplied by the factory as a group (garniture) in 1764

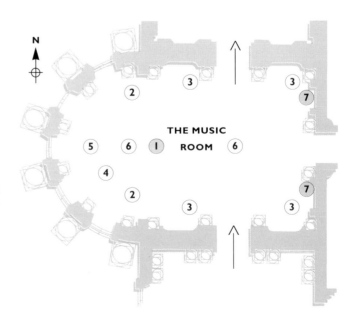

RIGHT: The Queen in the
Music Room with President
Nelson Mandela of South
Africa before a State Banquet
held in his honour, 1996

THE WHITE DRAWING ROOM

LEFT: The White Drawing
Room

The Royal Family gather here before meeting their guests in the Music Room. This was originally called the North Drawing Room; the pilasters were of Siena scagliola and the walls covered with gold and white figured damask. The present white and gold French-inspired wall decoration dates from the late nineteenth century. The ceiling survives as designed by Nash and combines a swagger tent-like composition with brilliant convex coving and delicate moulded plasterwork by Bernasconi.

William Pitts' twelve frieze panels depict the Origin and Progress of Pleasure and were described by the Parliamentary Select Committee into the financing of the rebuilding in 1831 as the 'sports of Boys'; they cost £800. The twelve individual panels are Love Awakening the Soul to Pleasure, the Soul in the Bower of Fancy, the Pleasure of Decoration, the Invention of Music, the Pleasure of Music, the Dance, the Masquerade, the Drama, the Contest for the Palm, the Palm Assigned, the Struggle for the Laurel and the Laurel Obtained. The two white marble chimney-pieces after a design by Flaxman are particularly fine. The gilt-framed pier glasses were designed by Blore. One of them conceals a secret door from the Royal Closet through which the Royal Family enters the State Apartments on formal occasions. The capitals of the pilasters were designed by Nash and are a novel composition incorporating the Garter Star.

LEFT: Roll-top desk by Jean-Henri Riesener, veneered with fret marquetry and inlaid with trophies and flowers, c. 1775. Purchased by George IV in 1825

THE WHITE DRAWING ROOM

Like the other State Rooms, this contains magnificent French furniture acquired by George IV. The set of Louis XV armchairs is by Jean-Baptiste Gourdin. The most important object is the marquetry roll-top desk by Jean-Henri Riesener, which was bought by George IV in 1825. Almost certainly of French royal provenance, it is reputed to have been made *circa* 1775 for one of Louis XV's daughters at Versailles.

More garnitures of Sèvres vases can also be found here, these predominantly with a green ground. The four ebony and gilt bronze cabinets with *pietra dura* panels under Blore's large gilt-framed pier glasses are adaptations of cabinets formerly at Carlton House.

LEFT: HM The Queen by John Merton, drawing, 1989

PICTURES

1 *Queen Alexandra* by François Flameng, 1908

2 *François de la Mothe Fénélon, Archbishop of Cambrai* after Joseph Vivien, c. 1700

3 *Portrait of a Man in Armour* after Sir Anthony van Dyck, c. 1650

4 *Portrait of a Woman* by Sir Peter Lely, c. 1658–60

FURNITURE

5 Roll-top desk by Jean-Henri Riesener, veneered with fret marquetry and inlaid with trophies, flowers, etc, c. 1775; it may have been made for one of Louis XV's daughters; purchased by George IV in 1825

6 Set of French cabriole-legged armchairs by Jean-Baptiste Gourdin, mid-18th century

7 Piano by Sébastien and Pierre Erard in a gilded case painted in colours with *singeries* by Francis Richards, mid-19th century; bought by Queen Victoria in 1856

8 Four ebony and gilt bronze pier cabinets with early 18th-century *pietra dura* panels

9 Set of five chandeliers, gilt bronze and cut glass, English, early 19th century

10 Set of four French candelabra, gilt and patinated bronze, in the form of a faun or nymph holding cornucopia, late 18th century, on gilded wood pedestals in the form of cranes supplied by Tatham, Bailey & Sanders, 1811; made for Carlton House

11 Two pairs of candelabra, by Pierre-Philippe Thomire, gilt bronze, early 19th century; bought by George IV in 1813

12 French patinated and gilt bronze and white marble mantel clock, late 18th century

13 Two pairs of French patinated and gilt bronze candelabra, late 18th century

14 Two pairs of French late 18th-century patinated and gilt bronze candelabra formerly in the Old Throne Room, Carlton House

PORCELAIN

15 Vases, Sèvres porcelain, second half of the 18th century

16 Pot pourri stand designed for Brighton Pavilion by Robert Jones, incorporating an 18th-century Chinese celadon vase with *tôle peinte* elements and gilt bronze mounts by Samuel Parker and a marble base by Henry Westmacott, 1822–3

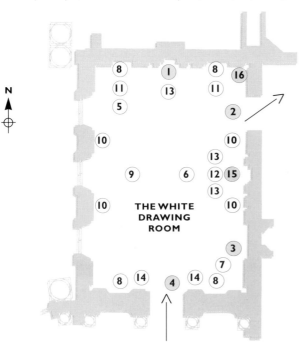

THE WHITE DRAWING ROOM

RIGHT: The Queen and
Prince Philip in the White
Drawing Room on the
occasion of their Golden
Wedding, 20 November 1997

The four French gilt bronze candelabra on carved and gilt pedestals, supplied by Tatham, Bailey & Sanders in 1811, come from the Crimson Drawing Room at Carlton House but are well suited in scale to this larger room.

The gilded and painted grand piano by Erard was bought by Queen Victoria in 1856 and is a reminder of her, and the Prince Consort's, love of music and the many concerts they held in the State Rooms, when new works by Mendelssohn and the elder Strauss were among the most frequently heard.

THE ANTE ROOM AND MINISTERS' STAIRCASE

RIGHT: Barograph in
mahogany and gilt bronze by
Alexander Cumming, 1765

BELOW: *Mars and Venus*
by Antonio Canova.
Commissioned by George IV
in 1815, one of three
sculptures by Canova in the
Marble Hall

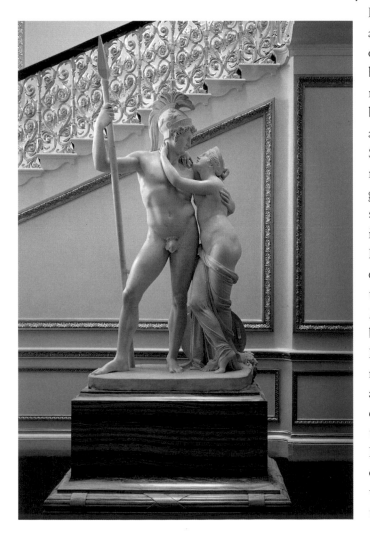

The Ante Room was contrived by Blore as a link between Nash's Picture Gallery and the new private rooms intended for William IV and Queen Adelaide but never occupied by them. It is given some distinction by its octagonal shape. After the grandeur of the principal State Rooms it has something of the character of a room on a nineteenth-century royal yacht, with its elaborate but small-scale decoration. The Victorian atmosphere is enhanced by the portraits by Heinrich von Angeli of royal princesses.

The Ministers' Staircase was also introduced by Blore, to give access to the monarch's apartments on the first floor and to improve the circulation at this end of the palace. The staircase was remodelled by Queen Victoria. A sign of Blore's more economical approach to the completion of the palace is that the balustrade is of gilt lead rather than the sumptuous bronzework chosen by Nash and George IV for the Grand Staircase. The space was redecorated in white and gold in 1902 as part of a sweeping renovation of the interiors of the palace by Edward VII. The late eight-eenth-century Gobelins tapes-tries are from the *Amours des Dieux* series and were bought by George IV in 1826. The English barograph in mahogany, kingwood and gilt bronze by Alexan-der Cumming is one of the few survivors of George III's original furnishings of Buckingham House. It was commissioned by the King in 1765, and

56

well represents George III's interest in clocks and scientific instruments.

At the foot of the stairs is an imposing marble group by the Italian sculptor Antonio Canova, commissioned by George IV (when Prince Regent) for the Circular Room at Carlton House at the time of Canova's visit to England in 1815. It depicts Mars and Venus. It is seen to best advantage from the Marble Hall, where it forms a focus at the north end. Canova was the greatest sculptor of the age, and George IV owned several examples of his work.

THE ANTE ROOM

PICTURES

1 *Princess Victoria Mary of Teck* (later Queen Mary) by Heinrich von Angeli, 1893

2 *Prince Albert* by Karl Schmidt of Bamberg after Winterhalter, painted on porcelain, 2nd half of the 19th century

3 *Princess Beatrice, Princess Henry of Battenberg* by Heinrich von Angeli, 1893

4 *Princess Helena, Princess Christian of Schleswig-Holstein* by Heinrich von Angeli, 1875

5 *The Duchess of York* (later Queen Mary) by Edward Hughes, 1895

6 *Princess Louise, Marchioness of Lorne* by Heinrich von Angeli, 1875

SCULPTURE

7 W. Reid Dick, *Bust of Queen Mary*, bronze, 1938

8 Harry O'Hanlon, *Family of the Horse*, bronze, 1988; presented to HM The Queen in 1990

9 M. Moch. *Two Loons (Canadian Sea Birds)*. green soapstone, 1990; presented to HM The Queen by the Prime Minister of Canada during the 1990 State Visit

FURNITURE

10 Two late 17th-century writing desks (*bureaux Mazarin*) veneered in tortoiseshell with *première*- and *contre-partie* Boulle inlays

11 Chest of drawers of Louis XV design, in kingwood parquetry with gilt bronze mounts

THE MINISTERS' STAIRCASE

TAPESTRIES

12 Two panels from a set of four, *Les Amours des Dieux*, woven at the Gobelins manufactory after designs by Joseph-Marie Vien, late 18th century; bought by George IV in 1826

SCULPTURE

13 Mowlm, *Five Inouits Tossing a Child*. green soapstone, 1977; a Silver Jubilee present to HM The Queen

14 Antonio Canova, *Mars and Venus*, c. 1815–17; commissioned by George IV following Canova's visit to England in 1815, it was delivered to Carlton House,

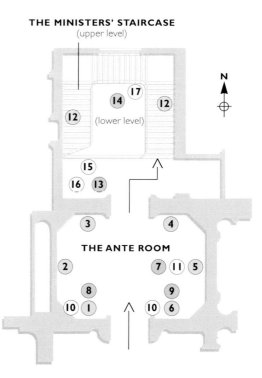

THE MINISTERS' STAIRCASE
(upper level)

(lower level)

THE ANTE ROOM

London, in 1824, where it was placed in the Gothic Conservatory

FURNITURE

15 French mahogany and bronze centre table with green marble top, 19th century

16 Barograph by Alexander Cumming, mahogany and gilt

bronze, 1765; commissioned by George III and delivered to Buckingham House at a cost of £1,178

17 Barometer and pedestal, attributed to Jean-Pierre Latz, Boulle marquetry and gilt bronze mounts, c. 1735

THE MARBLE HALL

LEFT: The Marble Hall

The Marble Hall lies underneath the Picture Gallery, running from north to south of the main block. It was originally conceived at Lord Farnborough's suggestion as a sculpture gallery, repeating the arrangement in his house at Bromley Hill, Kent, which had separate sculpture and picture galleries superimposed. Its original architectural character was more austere, with plain scagliola walls as a background to marble statues. The floor and Corinthian columns are of Carrara marble and match those in the Grand Hall, to which it is spatially connected. The two small-scale marble chimney-pieces were probably brought from Carlton House when it was demolished. Here, as elsewhere, the later gilded decorations were added by Bessant in 1902; the carved and gilded wood swags above the fireplaces, which may be in part early eighteenth century in date, were placed here then.

Here can be found another fine work by Canova, the *Fountain Nymph with Putto*, which was originally commissioned by Lord Cawdor who, however, allowed George IV to have it when it was completed. The other marble nymphs were mainly commissioned by Queen Victoria and are by German sculptors: Emil Wolff, Carl Steinhäuser and Josef Engel.

The portraits were arranged here by Queen Victoria and are of some of her immediate relations – including her mother, the Duchess of Kent; and Ernest, Duke of Saxe-Coburg and Gotha, the father of Prince Albert. They culminate in official State Portraits of Queen Victoria and Prince Albert painted by Winterhalter in 1859. This series is one of a number of dynastic portrait displays in the palace that were conceived by Queen Victoria and have survived unaltered down to the present day.

BELOW: King George VI investing Major Tasker Watkins with the Victoria Cross on 8 March 1945 in the Marble Hall

LEFT: *Fountain Nymph with Putto* by Antonio Canova, 1817–18, in front of *Augustus, Duke of Sussex* by Domenico Pellegrini, c. 1804

PICTURES

The official portraits of Queen Victoria and Prince Albert dating from 1859 are preceded by likenesses of their relations.

1   *Augustus, Duke of Sussex* by Domenico Pellegrini, c. 1804
2   *Victoire, Duchess of Nemours* (cousin of Queen Victoria) by Franz Xaver Winterhalter, 1840
3   *Ernest I, Duke of Saxe-Coburg and Gotha* (father of Prince Albert) by George Dawe, c.1818–19
4   *Victoria, Duchess of Kent* (mother of Queen Victoria) by Franz Xaver Winterhalter, 1849
5   *Prince Albert* by Franz Xaver Winterhalter, 1859; in the uniform of Colonel of the Rifle Brigade
6   *Queen Victoria* by Franz Xaver Winterhalter, 1859
7   *Charles, Prince of Leiningen* by Eduard von Heuss, 1841

SCULPTURE

8   Nielsine Petersen, *Christian IX, King of Denmark* (father of Queen Alexandra), 1906
9   Nielsine Petersen, *Louise, Queen of Denmark* (mother of Queen Alexandra), 1906
10 Antonio Canova, *Fountain Nymph with Putto*, 1817–18; commissioned by Baron Cawdor, who agreed to relinquish his rights

to it in favour of George IV. It reached Carlton House, London, in 1819
11 John Francis, *Ernest I of Saxe-Coburg and Gotha* (father of Prince Albert), 1846
12 Emil Wolff, *Sea Nymph with Trident*, 1841
13 C. Steinhäuser, *The Siren*, 1841
14 Eduard Muller, *Psyche*, 1861
15 Antonio Canova, *The Nymph Dirce*, c. 1814
16 Josef Engel, *The Nymph Clotho*, 1860
17 C. D. Rauch, *Queen Luise of Prussia*, c. 1817
18 William Theed, *Victoria, Duchess of Kent* (mother of Queen Victoria), 1861

FURNITURE

19 English carved and gilt gesso tables including two by James Moore, c. 1715; with a group of Japanese Imari beaker and baluster vases, 18th and 19th centuries
20 Spanish damascened steel table made by Placido Zuloaga for Alfred Morrison, 1880; purchased for the Royal Collection by Queen Elizabeth in 1938
21 Mantel clock by Benjamin Lewis Vulliamy, gilt bronze and biscuit porcelain, c. 1780
22 Pair of large vases, cloisonné enamel, early 20th century; given to King George V and Queen Mary by the Empress of China on their Coronation in 1911
23 Two from a set of four tripod candelabra by Bogaerts & Storr, 1807, and Morel & Seddon, 1826–8

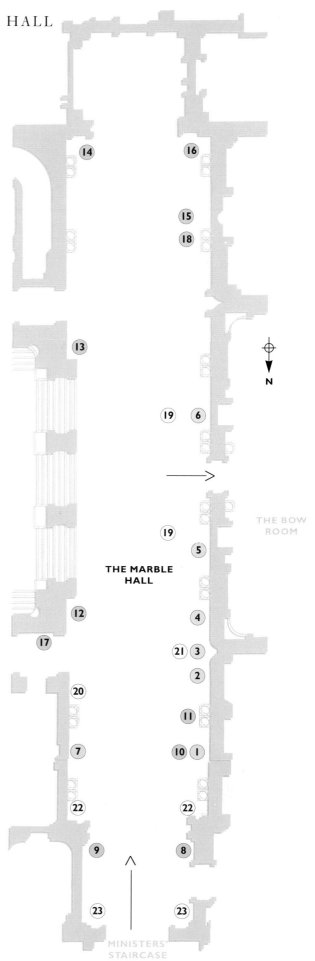

THE BOW ROOM

This room is well known to visitors to the Garden Parties as they pass through it into the gardens. Its more restrained Classical architecture with simple Ionic columns is typical of the semi-state rooms on the ground floor which were originally intended as George IV's private apartments. This was to be the King's library but was never fitted up as such. The pair of dark marble chimney-pieces with Empire gilt bronze mounts by Benjamin Vulliamy date from 1810. They were purchased by Queen Mary and inserted here, where they form a sympathetic counterpart to Nash's architecture. The oval portraits with gilt frames set into the walls were installed at the wish of Queen Victoria in

ABOVE: A plate from the Chelsea porcelain service presented by George III to his brother-in-law, the Duke of Mecklenburg-Strelitz, in 1763

BELOW: The Bow Room

THE BOW ROOM

1853. They are of European royalty related to the Queen, including the Kings and Queens of Belgium and Hanover.

The most interesting item in the room is the grand Chelsea dinner service commissioned by George III and Queen Charlotte as a present for her brother the Duke of Mecklenburg-Strelitz in 1763. At that time it was the most ambitious example of English porcelain ever made.

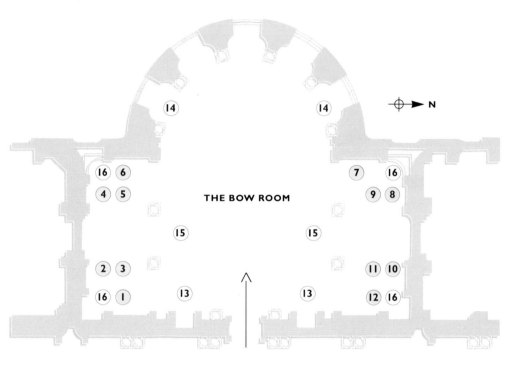

PICTURES

1 *Marie Henriette, Duchess of Brabant (later Queen of the Belgians)* by Nicaise de Keyser, 1854

2 *Ferdinand of Savoy, Duke of Genoa* by Eliseo Sala, 1853

3 *Augusta, Princess of Prussia (later Queen of Prussia and German Empress)* by Franz Xaver Winterhalter, 1853

4 *Ernest, Prince of Hohenlohe-Langenburg* by Franz Xaver Winterhalter, 1853

5 *Prince Leopold (later Duke of Albany)* by Franz Xaver Winterhalter, 1853

6 *Leopold, Duke of Brabant (later Leopold II, King of the Belgians)* by Nicaise de Keyser, 1854

7 *George V, King of Hanover* by Carl Oesterley, 1853

8 *Frederick William, Grand Duke of Mecklenburg-Strelitz* by Franz Xaver Winterhalter, 1853

9 *Princess Augusta of Cambridge, Grand Duchess of Mecklenburg-Strelitz* by Alexander Melville after Winterhalter, 1853

10 *George, Duke of Cambridge* by Alexander Melville after Winterhalter, 1852

11 *Princess Mary Adelaide of Cambridge (later Duchess of Teck)* by William Corden after Winterhalter, 1847

12 *Maria Alexandrina, Queen of Hanover* by Carl Ferdinand Sohn, 1853

FITTINGS

13 Two chimney-pieces by Benjamin Vulliamy, black marble with gilt bronze mounts, 1810; commissioned by the Earl of Bridgwater, they were acquired by King George V and Queen Mary

FURNITURE

14 Pair of English incense burners, mahogany, in the form of a covered urn on a pedestal, late 18th century; bought by Queen Mary

15 Pair of Regency inkstands, kingwood and gilt bronze, early 19th century

PORCELAIN

16 Service, Chelsea porcelain, 1763; presented by George III and Queen Charlotte to the Queen's brother, Duke Adolphus Frederick IV of Mecklenburg-Strelitz; presented to Queen Elizabeth in 1947 by James Oakes

THE GARDENS

ABOVE: Garden front

The gardens of Buckingham Palace, based on the original plans drawn up by William Townsend Aiton of Kew Gardens and John Nash, provide a walled oasis in the middle of London. George IV's and Nash's vision of the palace included its landscaped setting, with St James's Park on one side and these private gardens on the other. The principal feature is the artificial lake which was completed in 1828 and is fed by a conduit from the Serpentine in Hyde Park. The earth excavated was used to build an artificial mound on the south side which screens Buckingham Palace Road and the Royal Mews from the garden. The artful concealment of the boundaries makes the gardens seem larger than they are.

The Queen's Gallery at Buckingham Palace, where exhibitions from the Royal Collection are held each year, is closed for two years for remodelling and enlargement. It will open for The Queen's Golden Jubilee in 2002.

The Royal Mews, designed by Nash for George IV, are still in daily use and are opened to the public on a regular basis throughout the year.